Gay Romance

Short Story About A Husband Sharing His Wife For The
First Time In An FFM Encounter

*(Bundle Of Romance Novels Exploring Same Sex
Relationships)*

Reginald Jamieson

Van bolted from the house as quickly as he could. He stopped and cowered himself behind a skip as he heard sirens approaching. He trembled badly, wondering when the rush of adrenaline would subside. He was shocked to learn that he had murdered not one but two people. He had never imagined having to do it, but he did. However, they had threatened Tanner after robbing Parker. Something inside Van broke when the man on the stairs shot Tanner, for whatever reason. Like never before, his bear was roaring out of him. At that point, defending Tanner had been the only thing that mattered. It had overpowered him, but he didn't understand it. Compared to the man in the room who was attempting to apprehend Parker, killing the gunman had been a simpler task. Then he started to hear Tanner's ideas running through his mind. It didn't matter that none of it made sense at all. Until Van was certain Tanner was secure, he wasn't sure he would stop shaking.

The neighborhood was rocked by an explosion. Van realised abruptly what Tanner had done to hide their trail. "Tanner!" he exclaimed in his head, a yell ripping through his throat.

Tanner's voice echoed in Van's mind, "I'm okay."

Van stopped shivering a little when he realized Tanner was still alive. Even so, he hurried as quickly as he could to the van's location. He did not want them to be forced to stay in the area any longer than was absolutely necessary.

When they got to the van, Van changed to Human. In order to get Parker out of the backpack and prevent his temperature from falling too low, he swiftly put the bag between the seats, put on his clothing, got into the driver's seat and turned on the heater.

Parker rushed out of the backpack, climbed into the rear of the van and started to shift. As he sorted through the bags of items they had acquired up earlier while in Denver, Parker remarked, "Damn, that was scary." "Where are the clothes I purchased earlier in that bag?"

"Somewhere back there," Van answered. He peered out the window and into the mirrors, waiting for Tanner to come into view. He had an instinct that if Tanner returned to them, he would be able to unwind more. He had only spent a few hours getting to know the wolf, but he didn't want anything bad to happen to him.

Tanner is a really rough person. Parker let out a sigh and picked up the gym bag full of fresh clothing. "This is it."

"You are clueless. Without my stopping, he leaped out of the vehicle to pursue the Hummer you were riding in. Tanner's actions played a role in Van's decision to leap from the neighbor's roof into Parker's room. Before that evening, he never would have considered doing it. It seemed important to him to demonstrate to Tanner that he was willing to take risks as well. It had been terrifying to jump off the roof, but Tanner and Parker needed him. He had thus succeeded. After that, he tackled the man who was aiming at Tanner. Tanner was hit by the man on the steps, even though he was only a mediocre shooter with a pistol. Van realized he had to keep Tanner safe. He didn't want anything awful to happen to him, but he somehow suppressed the feeling. He was eager to learn more about Tanner. The wolf was drawing him in its direction.

"And tonight, he was shot." Parker climbed into the front seat and extended his hands towards the vent for the heater. He scowled. "I suppose my blue coat is missing. Though it wasn't the heaviest coat, I still thought it was extremely nice.

Tanner, still a big grey wolf, was scratching at the window before Van could respond. To facilitate Tanner's entry, Van unlocked the door and moved out. He let go of the bag, clambered into the rear and adjusted.

"Parker, could you please give me the trousers and leather jacket that are on the upper floorboard?" When Tanner was back in human form, he inquired. He complained a little bit during his shift.

Yes. Van sat back in the driver's seat, dropped Tanner's bag next to the one he'd made it out with, and Parker eagerly obeyed.

Are you alright? Van enquired. Tanner's agonising noises disturbed him. In addition, he had a slight itching in his hip as if he were sensing something other than his own discomfort.

"My hip still has a silver bullet in it." Tanner trembled a little. Hurts like an asshole's son. I must remove it as quickly as possible.

A great horned owl suddenly landed on the van's hood. A fat woman was standing close to the driver's side door a few seconds later. Van rolled the window down quickly.

Are all of you okay, Van? She looked in the window. "And Parker is back with you."

Yes, Virginia, we're doing well. Tanner, however, possesses a silver bullet. Van felt more at ease when he was with other shifters he knew. In Hardwood Valley, Virginia Comstock and her spouse operated a general store. They had been in his life.

Virginia winced. "You must return him home as soon as possible. Make an early call and ask your father to prepare Doc Sam. If we don't remove that as soon as possible, it will get poisonous."

Shortly after the appearance of another owl, Bob, Virginia's husband, moved to sit close to her. "You guys are to blame for the explosion and the resulting human excitement?"

"I reasoned that detonating the house would be a secure method to hide our tracks." Leaning over the seat, Tanner peered out the window.

Van's nose was assaulted with Tanner's strong wolf scent as he was only inches away from his face. It was almost too much to handle. Van want additional of it. He shook with excitement at it. When Van's phone rang, he reached beneath Tanner's arm that was leaning against the dashboard to grab it. His nose was less than an inch from Tanner's neck when he made the move. He considered kissing Tanner for a fraction of a second, but there were too many people in the area.

"You've returned to the van?" His dad sounded like a crazy man. "Is everyone doing alright?"

"Everyone is doing well. Bob and Virginia have also gotten through to us.

His father answered, "The others will be there soon." "There's a lot of chatter about the police and fire around here."

Yes, Van answered. That was us. We may not wait for the others to arrive because Tanner possesses a silver bullet.

"What?"

Virginia took the phone and reached through the window. The boys are returning, Hank. Here, we're going to take care of things and make sure that the humans have nothing on us. Prepare to locate this bullet and bring Doc Sam over to your place. Her eyes met Tanner's. "It doesn't look good for the wolf." Returning the call to Van, she did not wait for a response. "You guys return home." We can handle this.

Van picked up the phone and looked at Tanner. The faint layer of sweat that glistened on Tanner's face, down his neck, and dampened the dark hair that was visible on his chest through the opening at the top of his leather jacket zipper had escaped his attention since he had been preoccupied with how wonderful Tanner smelled.

His father gave the command, "Get your saviour back here if he's injured." "The others can follow Virginia and Bob's lead and observe what transpires in Rifle."

Will work. I'll see you shortly. Van didn't wait for his father to finish speaking. Before he turned to face Virginia again, he ended the call and replaced the phone in the cup holder;

Bob had already transformed back into an owl. Similar to fur, feathers provide significantly greater protection from the cold than naked skin did. "Thank you, Virginia."

She gave a headshake. "Our community is us. We cover one another's behinds. Parker is doing okay, that's all. Silent but functional.

Parker laughed. "I do know how to be quiet sometimes."

"I'll keep that in mind the next time you refuse to stop talking." Virginia chuckled. "You guys leave now. Preserve the wolf. After shooing them away, she transformed back into an owl, flew to the petrol station's roof and sat down beside Bob.

"Tanner, I'll try to get us home as soon as possible if you can settle back there." Van shifted into reverse and folded up the window.

As Tanner retreated from Van's seat and vanished into the rear, he cautioned, "Don't go too fast." "We don't need to end up in a ditch, and the roads aren't pretty."

Parker fastened his seatbelt. "He is correct."

"However, he's been shot," Van protested.

Tanner let out another painful noise, and vehicle felt compelled to accelerate the vehicle to reach the house. "The bleeding has slowed down thanks to the repositioning. I would have recovered by now if it weren't for the silver bullet. I may have an issue, but I won't pass out if we can't figure it out in a few hours.

And that was putting it mildly. Van let out a sigh. "In ideal circumstances, we can get to the house in about an hour." In an effort to avoid drawing notice from the authorities who were still rushing towards the hunters' house, he drove cautiously back to the interstate.

"We'll succeed." Parker reached for a chocolate package he had earlier hidden in the glove compartment.

Van thought Tanner was attempting to settle in when he heard some rustling from the bags in the back. He considered asking Parker to return there for a moment so Tanner could take the seat, but then he remembered that Tanner would not be able to sit comfortably at that point if he had been shot in the hip.

From Tanner came a low snarl. "I'll be alright. I'm a hard man. Please bring us there without incident.

"I'm going to." Van tightened his hold on the driving wheel and sped along the ice motorway. Before the silver caused too much harm, he was determined to bring Tanner to Hardwood Valley.

The stroll wasn't too long, which was fortunate. Malachai was dying to be with Johnny, but there was also something incredibly refreshing and strangely pleasant about being with him. It's similar like jumping into a chilly sea on a scorching day.

"Johnny, what are your thoughts on paranormal phenomena?" Glancing at him with his hand in Johnny's, Malachai followed the man to a little, dilapidated flat complex. "Have you ever encountered a werewolf or any similar creature?"

Although it was expected that Johnny would give him a strange look, the human responded.

"No, not when I was sober," he responded with relative ease. Unlike Malachai, who was curious as to why things were the way they were, Johnny seemed to take a lot in stride.

That's going to sound like a really strange thing. I had to try telling you, even though I doubt you'll believe me.

Malachai paused for a moment, then pulled Johnny into his arms and gave him a long kiss. He desired that kiss, even if it scared the human away. Malachai became somewhat sidetracked as Johnny melted so flawlessly into his arms.

His dragon warned him to shut up. His mate was Johnny. He refused to run. He couldn't and would never leave Malachai since the two of them belonged together. Their first kiss seemed to confirm everything his dragon had been saying, and it went on forever.

Upon the kiss's eventual breakup, Johnny turned to face Malachai, his lips swollen from the intense kissing.

"Believe you about what?" he inquired, and Malachai was relieved to see that Johnny shared her level of arousal and desperation. Malachai could feel Johnny's erect cock against him as he leaned in closer, and that sensual, seductive purr of a voice was deeper than normal.

After entering his flat, Malachai inhaled deeply and dragged Johnny in the direction of the bed. He was impatient and sensed that his incredibly attractive small partner was also impatient. Is he really so fortunate? To have discovered his soul mate, and for him to be so exquisitely gorgeous?

"I'm distinct from other men. I can make you if I take you. Malachai gave a headshake. He had never given it much thought as to what it might be like to share this with a person. After all, he had always been so cautious. "I could conceive you," I am aware that you are a man, too.

When Johnny turned to face him, the cutest, most contemplative expression appeared on his face. Most people wouldn't even consider such a thing, but Johnny was not like that.

Slowly, Johnny remarked, "I think that I drank more than I thought."

Malachai pushed Johnny onto the bed, gently but firmly.

"Yes, I realise that I sound crazy," he admitted before shaking his head. "Remember that I tried to tell you, just in case it happens and if I'm right."

Johnny was not convinced by him. Who among us would? However, Johnny's response was far more subdued than Malachai would have imagined. Aside from being his mate, this young man was something else entirely.

Johnny said, lying beneath Malachai and looking up at him, "I don't get the joke." They were both frantically ripping off each other's clothes as they conversed. Now that Malachai realized this, nothing could stop it. Nothing. It was inevitable. Although the conversation ought to take place prior to the undressing, Malachai was in dire need of it.

"It's not a joke," Malachai muttered, surveying Johnny with utter disbelief. The man was really attractive. tight, muscular, and toned, with wide shoulders and a narrow, slim waist. He was exactly the perfect example of a Malachai.

Johnny let out a faint grunt as his hand encircled Malachai's penis. He had truly attempted to warn the human. His dragon had been yelling at him to grab the human and claim him, so it hadn't been easy either. His ability to even attempt it had been something of a minor miracle.

He snarled and pressed his nude body up against Johnny's. The human extended his limbs in his favour, and whatever transpired between them, it was sensed by others besides Malachai. He could tell by the eagerness with which Johnny exposed himself to him.

Johnny muttered, "Malachai, take me, I need you," and it was exactly as Malachai had anticipated. Nothing on the earth could prevent him from following Johnny's request.

Malachai snarled gently, "Mine," and then forced Johnny's compliant legs apart. He positioned himself and paused for a split second, just long enough to consider whether or not to proceed.

Naturally, there was no other option. Not for Johnny, not for him. In actuality, Johnny belonged to Malachai, but that didn't work both ways.

The whole incident had an air of inevitable consequence. Malachai was aware that he was far from prepared to become a father. How could he be one when he hadn't even known one growing up? However, in the end, all that mattered was that this was his partner.

Malachai exerted pressure. With the human's entrance tight and heated around him, he slid within Johnny. Like he'd heard what the stories had described, Johnny was readily accepted by his body. It felt as though Malachai belonged inside him and they were designed to be together in this exact way.

But Malachai could never have envisioned how much more intense sex could get from the whole mate issue. He let out a moan and tightly hugged Johnny, who was also clinging to him, sensing the heat from his partner's perspiration and their desperate attempt to unite as one person.

Malachai felt a frightening wave of possessiveness as he stared down at

Johnny, at his mate. He was his. His dragon took control as he looked down at him, and a wave of tremendous heat engulfed him, manifesting as bright orange flames.

Naturally, he was having an orgasm at the time, which is why he was unable to control it. He quickly put out the fire once more, but it was too late. The instant he saw the black lines, which were too clearly visible on the light blue, seared into Johnny's blankets, he knew that.

The fact that Johnny arrived before to the fire was the sole bright spot. Malachai's body was still covered in heated traces of it.

Nevertheless, Malachai would have long since moved past any doubt that

Johnny was his mate. Though afraid, Johnny was unburned by the flames. Only if Johnny were genuinely and completely bonded to him would that be possible.

Malachai remarked, his voice low and unexpectedly courteous, "I just made you pregnant." It was a significant event.

Johnny looked around at the charred bedding and shook his head.

"I am unable to handle this. I am unable to. Upon observing Johnny's gaze, Malachai was forced to concede that was most likely the case. Johnny's world had never experienced anything like this. It was evident from his behavior.

"Is it okay if I go?" Malachai was reluctant to go. His desire was to remain and tend to his partner. His partner who was expecting. On this one, though, his human side was going to have to prevail against his dragon.

Malachai winced as Johnny mutely replied, "Yeah, I really do." He had thought that Johnny would require his presence in some way, but that was not the case. Here in his own flat, Johnny had no threat and he needed space.

"What day is it? I'll come if I'm free."

"This weekend."

After giving it some thought, I decided to treat myself and nodded. But Metatron didn't appear to notice, his gaze locked on the grass. I followed his gaze, seeing a flash of priceless light emerging from a few thin blades of grass holding beautiful feathers that were a blend of pale gold and silver.

Metatron held out his thumb and index finger and flicked the feather a little. "Haven't seen much of you lately."

I rotated the feather in my hand after picking it up. "You don't often leave the sanctuary, which is why. What activities have occupied you recently?"

"Lilith and Adam are both made. Eden setup is taking up my time. Metatron rested his elbow on his knee and made a strikingly elegant motion with his five fingers as he ran them over his short hair before reverting to the starting position.

"Are you serious? Thus, Eve not present?"

Metatronswiveled to face me, his eyes slitting as he did so. Have you been listening in on us, Isar? His Highness Lucifer insisted on calling her Lilith, even though I suggested the name Eve."

I was afraid that if I spoke one more thing, I might unintentionally change the entire history of humanity and make my future self disappear from the twenty-first century. But all of a sudden,

Metatronlaughed, his tone captivating. Subsequently, his second hand extended to grasp me firmly. "What have you been up to, you rascal? Why don't you visit me yet?"

I chuckled uneasily while shivering. Where was the mischievous child? "Well,

Metatron's palace isn't short of company, so one less won't matter, haha." Assist me in getting rid of this cheater!" But I've been missing you a lot recently." Metatron's eyebrows dropped, revealing a hint of unidentified bitterness. Before long, his big hand was running through my hair, cradling my head against his chest and drawing me even closer. "Isar, keep your distance from that person," he said in a quiet whisper.

He gave me goosebumps all over, and I gave a forceful shake of my head. "We'll talk about it on your birthday, I'm too hot right now."

I was still woozy from Metatron's affection when I passed out on the lawn after the stiff rehearsal. I let the gentle breeze play with the feathers and exclaimed, "Naughty kid—!" in desperation.

Like a caterpillar descending from the tree, Lucifinil landed on my legs like a tiny Spider-Man. With his petal-like face getting close to mine and his big blue eyes sparkling like sapphires, he crawled to my chest and tipped his head slowly down. My eyes grew wide as I gave him a gentle shove. He just stayed there, crawling over my head and exposing me in such a way that it was embarrassing.

"You vile person!Lucifinil, please return to me. I leaped to my feet and screamed at him, but he was already airborne, flapping his wings.

I had originally assumed that if he returned, I could simply go to the "Wings of Grace Café" and use the dishwasher. But as soon as I took off with my books, I became aware that my wing flapping had become more frequent. I therefore reduced my speed. However, the frequency didn't decrease. Yes, there was only one person who could make this particular kind of wing-flapping sound akin to a bee.

When I turned around, Lucifinil gave me a sly smile. "Where are you going?"

"I'm going to Heshbon City."

"To see Metatron?"

"Metatron's Highness lives there for six days?"

"How are you going to celebrate his birthday when you don't even know where his house is? In addition, he doesn't have a birthday for another six days, so he'll probably visit the Jerusalem villa."

"Why? Isn't this place better?

"He enjoys sensual women. Jerusalem's women are all incredibly passionate."

We flew by a cluster of dark blue buildings and had a conversation as we went. Every day, I couldn't help but wonder, "What is that place?" when I saw this unique building.

That's where Uriel lives. Do you know about the water curtain in front of the house? Look around; you may notice something truly remarkable."

"Is that the Thunder Mirror?"

"You know about it?"

"I've previously seen the Wind and Water Mirrors... It should be the Thunder Mirror because it's blue."

"Oh? How does one appear in the wind mirror?

"...No change."

Lucifinil appeared carefree. "After looking in the wind mirror, I noticed a noticeable difference. However, I don't think so."

It didn't seem real to me either. That being said, I couldn't resist taking Lucifinil and flying over when I saw the Thunder Mirror.

The person who has the biggest impact on a person can be seen through the Thunder Mirror.

The sound of clear water cascading down the blue stone pillar resounded like a sharp harp. Lightning struck through the water several times, fast and bright as shooting stars in an endless sky.

I noticed a sensitive face in the water curtain. a snow-white complexion, a head full of short, tousled curls that poked up here and there. This was a far too familiar face.

It was me. Alternatively, Isar.

The angel within, though, was naked, and his hands appeared to be gripping something as they faced the water curtain. He had four ice-blue wings on his back, as I could see upon closer inspection. His wings and hair felt a little wet at this moment, like he had just stepped out of a fog.

Speaking of mist, it appeared that we were surrounded by it.

The image got sharper and sharper, like a well-polished old film.

Strange, mystical electricity danced in front of me. The erratic patterns would cause a tremor in the heart with each flash. A few light crystal curtains floated behind Isar, as the water flowed gently behind her.

Abruptly, a curtain parted, revealing a picture-perfect face. Isar's eyes were pierced by a nose made of diamonds, eyes that flowed like waves, and a breathtaking, brilliant beauty.

I recoiled in shock, taking a step back unconsciously. What was happening?

This individual was... Lucifer?

All Lucifer had on was a flimsy robe, the hem of which flowed like Santa Filia's eternal smoke. His lips were lightly pursed, a delicate ribbon in his mouth, and his pale golden lashes shielded his eyes. Gathering his golden hair, he tied the ribbon around the silky strands that fell to rest against his chest. Isar moved his wings and went to tie it for him, seemingly indifferent to the fact that he was naked. A smile curved Lucifer's eyes, and they never left him.

Isar moved a little awkwardly, and after a few tries, his neck thickened and his face flushed. When he did manage to finish, the result was a tangled mess. He was about to untie it when Lucifer drew him in and held him tightly, their lips meeting.

"Why?" With a gasp, Javier's body contorted against the ropes. He felt extremely sensitive in every way, as though he would blow up in response to any kind of touch too soon.

"Because it wasn't torture anymore."

Javier was about to respond when Miguel pushed hard and quickly inside of him, filling every weak spot with his massive cock. With a silent moan of pleasure-filled agony, his mouth opened wide, his toes curled, and his eyes rolled. It was simultaneously too much and insufficient. All he knew was that he was always in need of more.

"What are you feeling?" Miguel questioned while rubbing Javier's wrists.

Even though he had been off the ropes for some time, he had wanted to wait to stop until he was completely healed. Before retreating even deeper inside Miguel's embrace, Javier extended out from under them.

"Excellent," he muttered. "I feel wonderful." He also meant it. He had never felt so whole as a person, whether it was a shifter or not.

Miguel paused his text conversation and bent down to give Javier a kiss on the lips by tilting his face upward. "It wasn't overly harsh?"

Javier gave a headshake. He assured, "It was just the right amount."

They briefly fell silent once more, focusing more on "what next" than the sexual activity. Was Javier returning to his native Miami? Did he intend to stay? Would Miguel accompany him?

Miguel finally said in a whisper, "I guess we should talk about this." He gave no explanation. Javier understood what he meant, he knew.

"How could we not?" Javier questioned while contorting to make it easy for him to see Miguel's face.

"Explain what you mean."

Javier clarified, "I mean, what if we didn't talk about it." "How about we just approach things day by day and see where they take us? Surely, we are the only ones present here? Why then do we need to establish our identity?

Miguel realized he was right. Is it what you're hoping for? He enquired.

Javier bent forward to plant a kiss on his jaw. He uttered, "I know that what I want right now is you." "Is that sufficient?"

Miguel grinned and gave a head nod. Yes, sweetie. That's sufficient.

"It's too much for me."

With a heavy heart, I withdrew myself from him. Lucas passed out as soon as I let go of him and began to gasp for air. Spit trickled down his chin and onto my bedroom carpet, and he coughed to clear his throat.

I said, "Have you had enough?"

With teary eyes, he glanced up at me and shook his head.

I said, "Present yourself."

"Yes, master."

He nodded to me and straightened up. He removed the t-shirt that was underneath his hooded sweatshirt. His physique surprised me a little. a broad shoulder paired with a muscular chest. A row of hair just above his navel and a six-pack on his stomach. His body bore some interesting scars.

Odd...

I was unable to think about them further due to my desire.

Between his legs was a small but swollen cock that was visible when his jeans and knickers were combined with the rest of his outfit. I petted myself and saw him get down on all fours onto the bed.

I stepped in behind him and drew nearer to him. To get a better look at him, I spread him open and gripped his ass cheeks. Slick Omega Fluids was prepared and waiting to make his entrance. But I made the decision to take my time now that I knew he was willing so much.

I said, "Do you want it?"

"Yes, that's what I want."

"Ask for it."

Please. I'm interested in it.

"What do you want?"

"I desire that you fuck me." Alpha, I want you to fuck me.

I cocked towards his opening. When I pressed my tip against his entrance, he sighed. My cock was pulsating with anticipation due to the wetness on its tip. I didn't enter him, though. Not just yet.

"Do you really want this?" I enquired.

"Yes, please, I want it."

However, this is your first encounter with a jaguar. If they learn what you've done, what will they say about you?

"I'm not concerned."

"What do you not care about?"

He spun around and gave me a look. The desperation in his eyes was visible to me. An hour ago, he might have been a stranger to me, but for tonight at least, he was an Omega, my Omega.

"Alpha, fuck me," he exclaimed. "Fuck me like I'm yours—Ahh!"

I cut him off by shoving my cock inside of him. I couldn't resist. The slick walls of his asshole were enough to make both of us lose focus.

I gripped his waist and proceeded to bang my cock into him as deep as I could. He groaned in pleasure with every hard thrust.

"Yes," he grunted. "Just… like… that…"

He could barely get the words out as he tried to breathe.

There was nothing more satisfying than having an Omega at your mercy. That feeling of erotic desperation couldn't be emulated by anything else. It was the only thing that could make me forget about everything else going on in my life.

I squeezed my hips tight around his waist and started to lose control of my own thoughts.

The pleasure was starting to burn hotter inside of me. My muscles tensed. Sweat dripped from every inch of my skin. My grunts grew shorter.

Watching the sweating man in front of me take my cock was like something out of a dream. His muscles glistened underneath the moonlight shining in through the windows. I was desperate for any sort of release and so was he.

"Do you want me to come?" I enquired.

"Y-yes, sir," he stuttered. "Come inside of your Omega."

"Say please."

"P-please…"

I smirked at his response.

My grip tightened on his waist until I was banging my body harder than I'd ever done it tonight. The sound of my hilt slapping against his ass grew louder.

"I can't take it! I can't take it!"

He cried out to me as he collapsed on the bed completely, his ass still up and presented to me.

Suddenly, his body started to tremble. I felt his walls tightening on me, squeezing the life from my cock.

I held onto his waist and gripped hard then found my release.

My cock throbbed, deep inside of his asshole, as I started to come. I let out a roar loud enough for all of Dirge to hear. Thick pulses of cum made my entire body shake violently. My whole body was going numb with pleasure.

I spilled every drop of cum deep inside of him. As my orgasm started to subside, I finally felt his asshole release me from his grip. I did the same for his waist with my hands.

My cock fell out of him, wet and shining with a combination of our fluids. I let out a deep and satisfied sigh before collapsing on the bed.

As I laid there with my head on the pillow, staring at the ceiling, Lucas took his place next to me. He leaned up close to me and kissed me on the chest.

"Alpha..." he whispered.

I looked down at his face and saw him smiling.

"Omega," I said.

As my eyes shifted down, I saw just how much pleasure he had endured. His small cock was wet with some of his cum leaking from it into a small pool on my mattress.

I didn't care that he came. I never cared when an Omega came. My only concern was that he'd given me what I wanted, just like all Omegas should.

"Two gold pieces," I said. "I said I would give you two gold pieces."

"I remember. I don't intend on asking for more."

Alright. You'll realize then that I'm not done with you.

He lifted his head and gave me a glance.

I said, "If I came inside of you only once, I would bring shame to my lineage." "I plan to get the best value for my money."

He smirked and answered, "Of course." Give me a moment, please. I must heal.

His head landed back on my chest. I gave him a gentle touch on the back of his head, sighing with satisfaction.

The night was far from over.

He asked, his eyes glaring, "What do you think you're doing here?"

"Why am I in this place?" I said, a little perplexed. "I'm just sitting here sipping my beer,"

"Are you not aware of who you are speaking to?"

I shook my head and blinked at it.

"I apologize," I said. "I fear that I do not."

"You don't, of course. You would be wise to avoid entering such a place.

I noticed some males leaning against the wall and staring directly at me when I peered over the man's shoulders. There were four of them, and their expressions were all the same. They seemed to be simply waiting to destroy me.

The bald man smelled as he leaned in close to me.

"Jaguar," he smirked and replied. "Your kind doesn't come around here very often."

His abrupt interruption had diverted my attention so much that I had not had time to look closely.

I only needed to smell him once to know exactly who he was.

A hyena. There was an odor about them. It smelled strong. You could have choked on it due to how intensely it filled your nostrils.

He took a step toward me, but I held my ground.

He asked, "Do you know what we do to jaguars around here?"

I gave the man a backward look. Even if his pack was immediately behind him, I wasn't going to back down.

"I am an Alpha," I declared boldly.

He laughed at me, then scoffed.

There are a lot of Alphas in this room. Not quite jaguars, but still Alphas. Examine your surroundings. Do you really believe that wearing an elegant suit and sticking your nose up will win you respect from me?

"What is it that you want?" I stated.

I spoke up. I made enough noise for everyone in the little bar to turn and pay attention. All around me, the chatter became quiet.

"Donovan."

Andrea tried to yank me away with a hand on my arm and murmured to me. She was a Beta who was constantly attempting to mediate conflicts. It must have been difficult for her to move between two Alphas, in my opinion.

With his eyes fixed on me, the man snarled to Andrea, "Shut up, bitch." "I deal with the jaguar in business."

I said, "You and I don't have any business."

Yes, I do. As you can see... You came into my bar. This is it. This is the domain of Black Stone.

"Ebony Stone?"

That's accurate. Our clubhouse is located here. Furthermore, I don't recall inviting you.

"I can't remember requiring an invitation."

Andrea gave me a strong enough arm tug to move me. She begged me, and I stared at her.

"Donovan, please."

Not that I came to Pandora to pick fights. I'm here to lend a hand. This hyena of a man in front of me didn't seem interested in anything. I made the decision to give up.

"I'm sorry," I said. "My friend and I are heading over."

He stopped me as I turned to go.

He uttered, "Ah, ah, ah." "Not quite that quick."

He stepped forward, keeping me from getting to the doorway.

"You entered already," he remarked. "You must now pay the toll."

"The price?" I inquired.

Indeed. For consuming alcohol at my bar without being invited.

"And what's the price?"

The man gave me a long, hard stare. A grin appeared on his face.

"Quintuples of gold," he declared.

"What?" Andrea shouted. "Five gold—"

"It's okay," I said, raising my hand.

I searched in my pocket for the gold and reached inside my jacket. I inserted the gold into the man's extended hand. He closed his palm over it, his smile growing even larger.

I said, "I'm sorry for entering your area without permission."

I was screwed. Really messed it up. I turned to face him again, my expression neutral. This young omega was getting hot, or I was really misinformed. I could see the signals, but he plainly didn't know, having never experienced it before. not to mention the aroma. An omega in heat had a distinct scent. I'd heard that a fated mate's presence may intensify things. Hell, I had witnessed it when Jude had saved Aiden the previous year.

Therefore, I was to blame for Ryan's suffering throughout this first heat, and I would also be to blame if I failed to support him during it.

Alright, settle in. After eating, everyone feels better. I sat down next to him on the blanket and grabbed a sandwich.

Ryan shifted erratically and had an uneasy appearance. At last, he muttered, "Thanks," and grabbed a pack of cookies. He didn't eat much, though. He had a flush and his brow was shiny with perspiration.

With a groan, I set my sandwich down. Neither was I hungry. Not for food, that is. With a shout of delight at having found his mate and the opportunity to impregnate him, my wolf was ravenous. It makes sense why so many of us were present. However, I really, truly wanted to avoid becoming instinctive and primitive. I had always taken pride in my ability to maintain self-control and to direct my own life's path. Not now, I thought bleakly.

"Ryan, are you feeling sick?"

He looked up, taken aback. "I believe I'm just suffering from a mild cold." I will attempt to withhold it from you.

I gave a headshake. "That's not the concern I have." He was a wolf shifter, after all. We were not sick often. That even an Academy omega ought to know.

I inhaled deeply. Ryan, I believe you're about to get hot. Consider it. I needed him to acknowledge it, so I didn't tell him I could smell it.

His expression was one of bewilderment. I haven't experienced heat, though. They suggested that I was a failure and that I must be infertile. Glancing downward, he again tugged at the opening in that accursed cover with his fingers.

I swallowed a remark. I used to be patient with everyone else. I have to quit being impatient with him because of my anger. "Well, perhaps the idea of being used in that way made your body become inactive." Once more, I reached for my sandwich. "I've heard that is possible."

His look was one of fear. "However, the reason I'm getting hot is because..."

With regret, I nodded. "Your body knows who your destiny is."

"Yes, indeed," he muttered. You don't want me, though.

He was simultaneously correct and incorrect. Even though I was incredibly hot for him, I wasn't going to allow my cock control my thoughts.

I gave a headshake. Ryan, it's not that I don't want you. That is, I have no desire for a partner at all.

Even though he must have understood that, he appeared as though I had struck him.

"I should not have traveled to locate you." He whispered softly. "I ought to have stayed away," My wrath was melting into sympathy for him, and I could hardly hear him. I struggled to gather myself.

I worked as a police officer. I was icy and rigid. I was aware of the dark side of life and the vulnerability of those who became involved. Even though I wanted to stay outside, I could feel my resistance waning.

I took a peek. Once more, he was fiddling with that blasted blanket. Once more, I had to hold back a caustic remark. Nothing had prepared me for the sudden flood of need that illuminated my imagination as his tiny frame was bent down. He was stunning. slender, malnourished, dirty, odorous, and unshaven. He was stunning, and I shed a tear or two knowing that I would have to do everything in my power to support him while he endured this heat.

The worst ones were always the initial ones. Not a good time ahead for him. I surveyed the open space. Although I doubt I have all we would need for a few nights, it would work as a sort of camp.

His eyes were blurry due to the fever as he looked at me. "What actions should I take?"

"Hold on there." I got up and headed for my truck. After a quick search, my worries were confirmed. I had my backup tarpaulin, which doubled as a bivvi tent in an emergency. Along with my four-season sleeping bag, I had a groundsheet. Ample water and a few MREs.camping supplies and a single change of clothes. But aside from a few Tylenol in the first aid bag, nothing can lower an omega's fever while it's hot outside. No additional sleeping bag, no freshly laundered clothes for him, and no adequate, actual laundry facilities. Additionally, it would be preferable if we moved closer to Blakestown. I turned around, having made up my mind.

Alright, Ryan. I believe it would be best to continue driving for a little while. While we drive, you can take a nap on the back seat while I pull my sleeping bag out. Before we set up camp for the night, I can then make a trip to pick up some additional supplies and clothing.

With bright, optimistic eyes tinged with anxiety, he nodded. He was aware of the risks involved with this heat, I realized.

I wrinkled my nose as I understood that after this, the sleeping bag would require a thorough cleaning and carefully tucked him into it.

"Yes, I understand that you feel hot, but you should remain covered up when you have a fever." I disregarded his protests, and he eventually backed down.

I thought uneasily that I'd have to cease being such a dominating demon. However, I had been exercising control over this for a very long time.

We quickly made our way back to the highway along the track. After giving it some thought, I turned back east. Really, I didn't want to go back, but I thought I had seen a hunting store a few miles ago, and I wasn't sure how far another one was to the west.

After thirty minutes, I arrived at the parking area. "All right, Ryan, just remain here. I'll get on it as soon as I can and lock the truck.

He seemed perplexed as he nodded. He had been sleeping uncomfortable, and I felt bad for waking him up. Still, there was nothing to be done. Thanking God there was enough of money on my card, I hurried into the store with a solid list of everything I wanted.

It didn't take me long to pack my purchases into the trunk. However, I turned off the GPS tracking on my phone before I started walking again. The store owner noticed me traveling east, which made me happy. That would confuse any people who follow you. I turned around and rejoined the road at the next intersection, going across the opposing carriageway.

Ryan had moved the sleeping bag back to allow himself to breathe in more cool air while he was still asleep. His appearance was considerably worse, and his heat had an unpleasant smell. I grimaced. It was not going to be simple. I started the lengthy drive to see how far I could go before we had to come to an end.

Tim, Jonathan, and Alec were invited to Alpha Nash's office in the main pack house on Sunday afternoon for a strategy meeting. Regular workdays would be the time for strategy talks, but on Monday, Alpha Nash would be heading to the Waters Edge Pack to meet with Alpha Sauk Yazzie to talk about territorial potential in the area.

Tim encouraged Jonathan, "Go ahead and tell them your good news; I think it is relevant."

Jonathan began by thanking everyone for taking him out to dinner the night before and for accepting him into the pack. He cautiously scanned the gathering before saying, "I know this is going to sound crazy since I just arrived, but I am pretty sure I met my fated mate last night at the Metro."

Alec snapped back, "I thought you seemed a bit anxious." "I was pretty anxious, especially after I accidentally knocked over my chair and struck Tim in the head with my elbow, but I was completely unprepared for it." "Me too," a beaming Tim replied. Jonathan said to his three new pack members, "I grew up hearing that a wolf could physically sense and smell their fated mate and I did."

"Who's that?" Alec enquired. Tim interrupted, saying, "It was our server, Joel, from last night." "I've seen him around our pack house on multiple occasions, but I know he's not one of our pack."

Alec explained, "That's because he is one of Chase's close friends."Joel and

Chase used to get together to prepare for tests. They were in the same university nursing cohort. During the summer, they will be working together to prepare for the state registered nursing exam. Alec surmised, "I presume he'll be back in our pack house studying with Chase. "This is excellent news," Alpha Nash remarked. Jonathan was congratulated by all.

As Jonathan has arrived, one of the reasons I need to meet with you today is to talk about how we will implement our new health care services. Alpha Nash made an effort to get as much information as possible from both his pack physician and his two betas.

"Tomorrow, I have a meeting with Alpha Sauk Yazzie from the Waters Edge Pack to talk about how we might work together to provide healthcare services. Your information regarding Joel's relationship with Chase could prove advantageous. Is there anyone who knows to which pack he belongs? Alpha Nash enquired.

Alec remarked, "I think he's part of the Terra Firma Pack." I could ask Chase after our meeting is over.

"I'd be grateful, Alec," Alpha Nash remarked. "It might not be good news if he is a part of the Terra Firma Pack."

"Why?" Jonathan questioned carefully.

"All right, let me run this plan by you. Alpha Nash stated, "One of the many reasons the pack funded Chase's nursing education was to enable him to join the pack's medical staff.

"I believe that by sending Joel to nursing school, the Terra Firm Pack is working toward the same objective. A medical crew is necessary on pack grounds. But having a link to human hospitals would be helpful if we needed shifter care off pack lands. Given that Chase is a human, we might ask him to work at a human hospital in addition to the pack to create a medical staff that is accommodating to shifters. We could have a robust program that could help all three packs if we could convince Alpha Daniel of the Terra Firma Pack to let Joel work on our medical team full-time, said Alpha Nash.

"Persuading the Terra Firma Pack to accept Joel into our new inter-pack medical team could be our biggest challenge. "What are your thoughts?" inquired the Alpha. Jonathan volunteered with haste, "Well, I would be more than happy to meet with you and the Terra Firma Pack Alpha." Jonathan said with a cunning smile, "Of course, I have a vested interest in the positive outcome of such an agreement."

As we move forward, it could be a good idea to talk about pack politics and history to keep Jonathan informed. Alpha Nash turned to face Tim and said, "I'm not sure how much Tim has told you about how the three adjacent packs emerged from the Eastern Shore Territory. Tim shook his head in disbelief.

Three groups of people lived as the Eastern Shore Shifters Pack along the mid-Atlantic coast about fifty years ago. There was an uneven distribution of alpha, beta, and omega wolves within the sizable pack. While each wolf performed important but distinct duties in their packs, some wolves felt that they should all be treated equally by the Federation of Wolf Shifters. They also thought that certain shifters might be able to locate their destiny partners among humans. The Timber Ridge Pack was created by this group, Alpha Nash went on.

"The second group had similar views to the previous group, but they disagreed that shifters and humans should mate regardless of any potential animosity between them. Because they believed that wolf shifters should never be discovered by humans, this group founded the Waters Edge Pack.

The Terra Firma Pack was finally constructed by the last group. This pack, which was fewer in number, held the traditional view held by our elder councils that wolf shifters need to live traditional lives. According to their beliefs, alphas are the most significant wolves and were created to both guard and populate packs. This pack's betas are just there to keep the group safe under the alpha's leadership. Omegas are the lowest type of wolves and are only here to fulfill the requirements of their alphas, procreate, and care for their young.

Tim questioned, "Who decided how the pack land should be divided among the three new packs?"

Alpha Nash went on, "The Federation was asked to negotiate and chart the new pack lands by the alpha masters from each new pack. The three alpha masters concurred that the three packs should receive an equal share of the area. The land's division was decided upon by the Federation, and it hasn't changed since. The main border between our pack and the Waters Edge Pack is shared from west to east, with both packs' east banks reaching the ocean. With constrained bounds, the Terra Firma Pack would run perpendicular to the other two packs, from north to south. In the end, the alpha masters determined that no shifter could cross pack boundaries without the two packs' alphas' written approval. I made a commitment to strive toward fostering goodwill among the three packs when I assumed the role of alpha master for the Timber Ridge Pack.Alpha Nash came to an end.

"Today, there is a positive relationship between the Timber Ridge and Waters Edge Packs," Tim stated. "Exactly," repeated Alpha Nash. Tim made the observation, "But neither pack has a strong relationship with the Terra Firma Pack."

The good news is that Chase is organizing our one-year anniversary celebration, which will take place on Saturday here in the pack home.

Jonathan nodded in agreement as Alec grinned directly at him and said, "I think Joel Ryan has been invited and will be attending."

Tim remarked, "Given that you brought up the anniversary celebration, we should probably consider whether we need additional security since humans and members of other packs will be attending." Jonathan reminded the gathering, "We also need to discuss our desire to collaborate with the other two packs on health care services."

Jonathan was motioned to stay behind by Alpha Nash as the group started to disperse. Jonathan, I would like to bring to your attention a delicate matter concerning the Terra Firma Pack and its possible connection to your destined partner Joel. The Terra Firma Pack buys omegas from other packs who sell them, though I am not aware of many packs that still do this. Since the three factions split, this has been a point of conflict amongst our three packs. I'm sharing this with you in case Joel was bought from a different bundle.

"I am aware of the procedure," stated Jonathan. "Omegas were not valued by my previous pack, and once they were born, they were sold. His attitude was gloomy as he said, "I appreciate the information." The alpha stated, "We might encounter some opposition from Terra Firma's Alpha Master, Daniel Allen." But if that issue comes up, we will deal with it, Alpha Nash stated. "Please know that your new pack and I will be here for you at all times."

He approached the tower thirty minutes later.

"Hello," he gestured toward me.

With a quick nod, I covered my eyes with my sunglasses.

"Listen, I understand that you're busy, but I'd be happy to buy you a drink if you ever wanted one." You know, preserving my life in every way.

I nodded once again, sensing a smile expressing my true feelings.

Yes, that makes sense. Let's say it's around seven. Tonight is my free time. If that suits you, that is.

He grinned in return. "Tonight, seven works perfectly. Which phone number do you have?

When I told him, he immediately texted me and plugged it into his phone. He said, "By the way, my name is Stewart."

"Robert," I murmured.

"Okay, Robert, I appreciate you saving my life. "See you later," he said, turning to return to his buddies without saying anything else.

I was happy and couldn't help myself. It didn't have to last, even though I knew it wouldn't. I shouldn't get too excited because it was only a drink, in the end. It had no significance.

Besides, I was heterosexual. I had never before received instruction from a male. I mean, I maintained my body in tip-top shape and enjoyed a man's body just as much as most girls do, but that didn't mean I liked them. But there was something about Stewart that I found really endearing. It was just too difficult for me to pinpoint. There was a magnetic pull of sorts. There was more than simply the fact that I had saved his life less than an hour before that brought the two of us together.

Still, the odds were favorable. He was merely being a decent man and getting a drink for the man who had saved his life. It was definitely meaningless.

"Robert, may I be absolutely direct with you?" Stewart inquired.

"It's true that I like direct," I declared.

We had gone from one drink to two, then three, and some dancing at a local club, and eventually we had found up back at his downtown apartment just after ten o'clock. Living on the top floor of a high-rise with a view of the whole city, Stewart seemed to be well-off. I had to decline his offer of a nightcap because he had made it. Not that I particularly wanted to. Stewart was witty, hilarious, and a phenomenal dancer.

We were enjoying the large bay windows in his living room while seated on his couch. In front of us was a glass coffee table. Our two scotches (Macallan 18-year, Ice Rocks) were placed on drink coasters on the table.

"I wanted to properly thank you for saving my life," said the speaker.

I said, "I was just going about my business, and you bought me drinks."

Indeed, but I believe you are deserving of better.

"What were your thoughts?" I asked, gazing into his large, stunning blue eyes.

"Oh, yeah, I was considering blowing a kiss to you."

I chuckled. There was no way I could have heard him correctly. Unless. Did I?

"Are you telling the truth?"

He chuckled. "I am, of course. You think I'm attractive, for sure, and I think the same of you. Unless... you've never?with a man previously.

I forcefully gulped. "I am unable to claim to have."

He grinned, but his face didn't look like a handsome man wanting to suck my dick; instead, it looked more like a shark.

So this will be even more enjoyable. If that's cool with you, that is.

"Yes, of course. Yes. Should you so choose.

"Oh, definitely," he replied, grabbing my hand and pulling me out of the room and down the hallway to his bedroom.

Stewart had a bedroom larger than my entire apartment, with a king-sized bed and large bed posts that reached the ceiling.

He gave the order, "Sit on the bed."

When I did, he knelt in front of me and stroked my crotch with his hands. He removed my belt and tugged at the sipper as soon as I felt my cock start to awaken. With ease, the pants slid down to my ankles, where my boxers fit in. Stewart grinned, staring at my dick with all of his concentration as my cock twitched.

He murmured, "Oh, a nice fat one," and began to caress it with his left hand. I exhaled and closed my eyes, savoring his deft handwork.

There was no doubt about that. Although that might have been my first time, it was unquestionably not his. His strokes grew faster, and then I sensed heat and something warm surrounding my cock. When my eyes opened, I saw Stewart with his mouth wrapped around my cock. He carefully moved his tongue around my cock head while I sighed and closed my eyes once more. He was stroking my cock, but at a slower pace than when he had first begun to fully animate it. He obviously was getting into it as he groaned while sucking and licking my dick head. His noises gave me the impression that he was in heaven, performing my first gay blow job.

My breathing became labored, and I reclined, instinctively reaching out to touch his shoulders with my hands.

In response to that, he became more positive and began to moan louder as he began to take more of my cock in his mouth, bringing its head up to the back of his mouth as he began to lower his mouth, inch by inch, onto my cock.

I couldn't resist taking hold of his shoulders and yanking him closer to my dick.

Stewart began to bob his head up and down on my dick, as if he was really getting into it, and he groaned and gurgled.

I moaned, "Fuck that's good head," which only caused him to quicken his pace.

Since I hadn't been that turned on in a long, long fucking time, I knew I wouldn't last long.

Well, who doesn't enjoy a good blowout, but this was just incredible. He had the exact same damn equipment that I did, so I suppose that helped. Stewart was just an expert at using his mouth, and you can't really pretend to be excited like he was with my dick.

Right now, my body is freezing, and I'm trembling while holding my phone and having no idea what I'm doing. I must have imagined whatever it was that happened. There was no possibility that the attractive college-aged biker guard had a ClickDesire profile. I thought, "No way," but then I reloaded the website and saw that his profile remained. I hid my profile because I wanted to end this before it was too late. It was really the only option available to me. The upside was that his pictures, which still showed him in his panties, were still visible to me. His physique was simply Jesus, I don't even know how to express this. With my hand slipping under my trousers and caressing my shaft, I asked myself.

His figure was tantalizing; the lines, curves, highlights, shadows, and pretty much every aspect of it seemed perfectly proportioned. Sliding my hands over his thighs, shoulders, biceps, and pretty much every part of him—including his prick—was exactly as I could picture myself. I knew it had to be large because of how massive his bulge was. I decided that my hand would feel so small compared to the thickness and length of his shaft, and then I would lower my trousers and use the lavatory.

I looked in the mirror, saw myself, closed my eyes, and started to jerk off. While thinking about Carwel mounting me and fucking me till he came inside of me, I wished that it would happen and knew that it probably wouldn't. I might even get pregnant with many of his offspring.

I coughed into the toilet, picked up my phone again, and collapsed onto the bed as the night outside grew quiet and the crickets began to sing. I felt so much better after releasing myself, like I could look at his profile again without getting scared.

Since Carwel and I would very certainly cross paths again—especially after that embarrassing moment when he told me everything he could about the maths issue, including the solution—I didn't want him to know that I was on the app. He had studied civil engineering, which is something I never would have imagined.

I pondered what more I didn't know about his life, given that he'd been in it.

When I refreshed the page, his profile was still visible. His profile image was the only thing that had changed; the rest of the pictures remained the same. After looking at his profile one more time and seeing that it featured him with his friends from the biker club, I pondered why that was. That was to be expected—he was an Alpha MC member.

I understood that any connection with him would be challenging, and I wasn't really dreaming it might happen, given the setting, the biker club, his pals, and pretty much everything else related to it. It simply wouldn't.

Sincerely, all it did was make me realise how unachievable it was, I thought to myself before hitting an app button that brought my profile back online.

I frantically pressed my finger on the screen in an attempt to conceal my profile, but I soon realized it was too late.

Jesus. What on earth was going on? I questioned myself, thinking that this was all quite surreal. The app seemed to want to show Nokon my profile, which wouldn't be possible if it weren't sentient.

I bit my lower lip, deciding to do something wrong. I might as well bite the bait, since he had already seen my profile. I liked his profile and sailed right over it without thinking twice.

Everything seemed to be rolling down a hill like a snowball after that.

I clicked on the message he sent me right away.

Should I respond to it? I asked myself, immediately shutting off my phone. I could theoretically go on a date with him and no one would ever find out because I lived alone now and could do anything I wanted.

Even so, it would still be uncomfortable because his age was indicated on his profile. thirty years old. There was nothing I could do about the age difference, even if he was attractive and didn't appear to be as old as he was.

Even yet, the thought of hooking up with someone ten years my senior made my cock tingle uncontrollably at the moment. I should have been feeling calmer and my cravings satisfied by now, but that wasn't what was happening. I had already jerked off.

I turned the phone back on and took a big breath. Carwel must be thinking that I was experiencing some strange phenomena at the moment. We also touched legs following that time we had with him outside the Engineering Building. I fled because I had been experiencing warm shivers throughout my body.

Simply put, I didn't want anyone to see my semi-formal and assume that I was an infatuated mess who couldn't manage my cravings—even though, on sometimes, that was exactly the truth.

Hello, Carwel. How are you?

I was at a loss as to how to respond to his communication. I really wasn't going to, I decided as I turned off the phone once more and reached under the bed to locate my clock. I had to wake up early tomorrow morning or I would be late for my classes.

Normally, I would use the phone for that, but not this evening. I would most likely wear a hoodie to college tomorrow. Not that I wished Carwel had seen me, but it was the least I could do.

What did I really believe would happen, though—that he would never see me again—even after that? Finding the whole situation too ridiculous, especially for someone like me who didn't have the luxury of going through this without harming my schoolwork, I reasoned that there wasn't even another exit off the campus.

and my slumber as well.

I cursed myself as I covered myself with the blanket and looked up at the ceiling. Carwel now undoubtedly despised me.

As Drakka moved his palm over her silky folds and then into them, accessing her most private area, her body tightened and she moaned. His hand was rather hot at first, but as he skillfully massaged the sides, sending white sparks of ecstasy shooting up her body, his fingers barely touched her clit before her mind was finally silenced. Her body felt every touch and sensation as he fueled a raging fire of need inside her, and her thoughts vanished as she was overtaken by instinctive cravings. She groaned and felt her body stiffen, aching for release, but he persisted in his deft massage and caressing of the tender nub.

Drakka pressed a finger inside her moist opening and started kissing her more passionately, his tongue exploring her deeply. When he slid it in, she felt a rush of pleasure unlike anything she had ever experienced, even if there was a slight touch of pain. She let out a sigh and whispered his name as Drakka moved his fingers in and out of her. She bit her bottom lip, gripping his hair and pulled it roughly as she threw her head back, the overpowering feelings turning into whimpers and then into yells of delight.

When Drakka put a second finger inside, there was a brief but sharp pain that was immediately followed by a powerful surge of pleasure. Saniyah threw back her head and let out a long, loud cry, sounding like an animal in heat, as he drove his fingers in and out of her with increasing force and speed. She gave his hair a violent twist and mashed her lips to his, driving her tongue into his mouth. Drakka groaned and drove his fingers deeper than he had ever done before, kissing her. It seemed like he liked that.

She was starting to feel something, but she wasn't sure what it was. She felt as though there was a tremendous pressure inside of her that began little and seemed to be growing into something much bigger. She kept stroking him off as hard and quickly as she could, gazing into Drakka's eyes with a frenzied, crazed look. All he could do was smile while he pounded his fingers into her.

He said, "It's okay, my Angeliym." "Acquire the feeling. Give yourself over to the emotions.

Saniyah was at a loss as to how to comply with his request. She didn't know how to let go or give in to the feelings. The sensation that she was powerless over her own body alarmed her, but it was also an incredible pleasure.

When Drakka removed his fingers from her, she let out a disappointed whimper. She was itching for his touch, the fire between her thighs scorching hotter than before. for her to contain him. She pulled him down onto her as she lay on the ground behind him, her hands sliding out of his trousers.

Drakka asked her if she really wanted this, looking into her eyes as if to get permission. Saniyah was insanely infatuated and desperately in need. All she did was draw her dress up around her waist and encircle him with her legs. She was only made to want him more as Drakka smiled at her, radiating lust and a hunger that matched her own.

For the first time, he showed her his long, thick cock by reaching down and sliding his trousers down. Admiring it, Saniyah reached down and picked it up. She knew that having his cock buried deep within her would be much more satisfying than how his fingers had felt. Drakka groaned, her hands clasping his cock and caressing it. Leaning down, he bit and sucked on her firm nipples while her dress's sheer fabric allowed him to see them.

Drakka brought his lips to hers and gave her a passionate kiss that came from pure desire. She slipped her hands up to his back, massaging the firm muscles that pulsed beneath his skin, then released his cock. She arched her back and almost shouted when he finally pushed his cock inside of her.

The largest of him inside her yet caused a bolt of pain as he slipped his cock into her, but the rush of pleasure that followed was just as intense.

Drakkabraced himself on his arms above her, gazing down at her with a look of pure joy on his face as he started to slowly move his hips and slide his thick cock in and out of her.

As he began to pump his cock deeper and faster, her nails bit into his flesh on his back, causing him to experience extreme pleasure combined with a little twinge of agony. She craved more since the combination of the two sensations was euphoric and intense. He moved more quickly as she rocked her hips and tightened her hold on him with her legs.

Drakka gave in and started thrusting his cock deep, fast, and hard into her. Her sultry cries could be heard echoing across the lake, along with the sound of their skin slapping together. Saniyah had no idea a man could make her feel like this. Very enjoyable.

She felt that pressure rising inside of her again, and it was rising quickly. She tried to give herself over to it as Drakka had instructed, closing her eyes and embracing it. He moaned, crying her name as he repeatedly pressed his cock into her, hard, fast, and deep, and when she opened her eyes again, his face was twisted into a mask of crazed delight.

Drakka's eyes flashed a deep red, his body tensed and trembling. The shaking in his body became more noticeable as he repeatedly buried himself as deeply inside of her as he could. Saniyah observed that the blue bubble of light that had surrounded them earlier had returned, with a deeper, more intense colour as the red light shining in his eyes got brighter.

The pressure inside her increased to a crescendo as Drakka repeatedly rammed his cock farther and deeper into her, reaching her core like a wave coming in off the ocean. Subsequently, the dam cracked. Saniyah's body tensed and spasmed, and she flung back her head and cried out. Her orgasm raged through her like a huge wave breaking, causing her to twitch and jerk.

Saniyah's body still shook as she drove her claws into Drakka's back, making him grunt. She felt his cock throb as he shot his hot seed deep inside her, and a moment later, he shoved his cock into her pussy, touching the end of her.

He let out a cry that was part primal scream, half moan of pleasure, as her pussy continued to spasm in ripples around him.

Drakka's hot, sticky cum caused her to feel filled up, which set off yet another wave of pleasant sensations. With her eyes closed, Saniyah tossed back her head and surrendered to it. Her wings seemed as though they were growing out of her body on their own initiative, and she opened her eyes.

She gasped at what she saw.

Her fluffy white wings spread out and fell as far as they could as they both hovered around 10 feet above the earth. With his wings spread wide and dark as onyx, and with a leathery aspect, Drakka hugged her tightly. Clasped in that blue ball of light that had encircled them since their first kiss, they embraced one other.

He nibbled my lip. I felt the pain as I moaned into his mouth, enjoying his firm hold and powerful hands. After I opened my mouth, the Dragon King pulled my legs around his hips and raised me into the air. He lifted me to his bed and moved away from the wall. He threw me onto the down blankets and plush furs. He was on top of me while I laid there gasping for air.

I heard my helmet clatter to the ground and my garments shred. He took off my boots, belt, and leggings, discarding them like a feral animal ripping meat from its victim. I had only my loincloth on. I was exposed, under a man who was superior to me in every aspect—rank, strength, and height. He bit and sucked on my neck, consuming it with his lips and tongue. Heat waves bloomed where he touched me, radiating all the way down to my cock.

"Whoa!"

He pressed his hips against mine, causing me to sob at the slightest contact. He pulled my loin cloth away with one hand. He grabbed my wrists and pinned them to the bed when I sought for his garments. He gripped my wrists tightly and worked his way down my body with his mouth while I attempted to buck away, not sure if I was prepared for what was about to happen.

He licked and sucked on my nipple, grazing my shoulder with his tongue and lips before moving on. He touched my abdomen. His facial hair tickled my skin.

His mouth lowered itself till it found my cock's head.

"What are you doing?" Ick! I yelled.

My hands were crushed against the bed by him. My eyes snapped open. He let his tongue lick my entire shaft after sucking my cock into his mouth. I felt him release me with a pop. My penis quivered and throbbed, yearning for more.

"Aaah!" I sobbed.

I didn't receive any more. He seized my hips and threw my hands above my head. My face was covered in furs as I lay on my stomach after the Dragon King threw me over. I heard the tinkle of metal on stone and the sound of his belt dropping to the ground. Then the familiar whip of a loincloth being swiftly pulled away, and the sound of his trousers being hurled backward. Gritting my teeth, I peered at him over my shoulder.

Did I not feel angry with him? Did I not observe this man grow fangs and wings a few days ago? Both fear and desire made my body tremble. More than anyone I had ever felt, his skin emanated heat. He pressed his thighs up against mine, pressing me down into the furs with his hand on my back. I gasped. I felt my hardness pounding beneath me as I gripped at them and twisted them in my hands. Even though I couldn't see him anymore, I could still feel his strength.

He grabbed my behind with his other hand. There was something thick and

lengthy rubbing between my cheeks. I
could not help but arch my back. My
body had wanted nothing more than this
man, more than it had ever wanted a
woman. I was unable to think rationally
about my circumstances, my people, or
our approaching demise. My mind was
racing with ideas, but they were all
directed towards him.

For him.

Something smacked against
something else. I sensed the oil slick. He
had it in his hand. He started at my
testicles and moved his greasy fingers all
the way up to my ass. I tensed up and
tried to move away, but he pinned me to
the bed by pressing down on my back.
Slowly, one finger circled my hole. I was

sick of pulling at my muscles. I unwinded.

The finger entered my opening.

"Whoa! Gods!

Then he leaned over me, his lips pressed against my ear, his beard tickling my skin and his breath heated against my neck.

He pressed his finger further deeply into me and said, "Is this your first time with a man?"

It was against the law. It fulfilled every wish I had ever had. I wriggled to meet his chilly, grey eye directly. Looking into millennia was how it felt. He gently pressed his finger into me while he waited for a response. I gave a nod.

His nose wrinkled up. A flush appeared on his cheeks. The way he moved his fingers, the tightening of his muscles, gave me a sense of tremendous urgency. He gave me the appearance of a man who had gone weeks without eating. When he finally spoke, his voice sounded deep and fractured, like a stone fracturing.

He withdrew, saying, "I will be as gentle as I can, which is not very."

He took his finger off. His scorching hot cock rubbed up against my crotch. He moved closer.

"Aaaaagh!" I let out a cry.

A searing agony shot through my body. I scurried up against his cock and the furs. He moved closer, his girth and length filling me out.

My mouth tightened, but the pain eased into me as the warm, slippery oil sank into me. He was up to the hilt inside me with one last thrust. I groaned as he shifted his hips. This was unlike anything I had ever experienced; it was like having a man inside of me. He plunged into action. I bit my arm to get at it. I was filled, left empty, and then filled again by his member. I was a fighter. I had never experienced being controlled by someone else to this extent. I was able to turn and glance at him. He had chilly eyes. With each thrust, his abdominal muscles contracted. His ebony locks shimmered.

I think that watching him increased my desire for him and my desire for him to take me. He tightened his fingers around my hips. White-knuckled and nervous. He was restraining himself. With all this power, he was controlling himself to keep me safe. Heat surged across my face. I was clueless as to its meaning. Every muscle in his body appeared taut. He had noticeable veins on his arms. I was unsure of whether I wanted him to hold back or for how long.

Gritting my teeth, I turned around and faced below.

I groaned, 'Faster, your Majesty can go harder.

He didn't require any more prodding. He pulled my ass up to his hips by dragging it behind him. I buried my face in the furs. He continued to thrust into me, pounding me. My cock is brimming with want, and my ass is screaming.

"Aargh!" He bellowed.

With a strong leg, the Dragon King climbed up onto the bed. He thrust downwards. Something inside of me felt like the tip of his cock ran down it.

"Aaaah!"

I had the feeling that I could explode at any second after touching that region. Once more, he struck. I let out a happy yell. It went through my entire body. He struck harder this time. Throwing myself onto the bed. What is this? Do ladies get pleasure from this? He struck me repeatedly, the blows coming in closer and closer. The enjoyment persisted. I was nervous. I could be overcome by anything.

My claws grew, revealing a part of me in the heat of our love for each other. Now he was standing, knees bent, and putting so much pressure on me that I felt like his cock was about to pop out of my mouth.

The tightness of my hole seized him with an intensity he had probably never felt from anyone before, and I could feel the hairs on my face standing on end. It must have been because we were so consumed by our feelings that we didn't notice three hours had passed while I was milking his hot white seed. Even though it was almost ten in the morning, we didn't give a damn.

"I have so much more to do than this." His balls were rising, the shaft was growing, the head was swelling, and before I knew it, I was turning and letting him shoot straight into my gaping mouth, so I don't think he was going to have to. I continued to be on my knees as I caressed his long Johnson and enjoyed every last inch of it. Even though he was groaning and had his eyes closed, I continued to lick his head after he was finished. I was aware that he would be sensitive, and he attempted to push me away—which was never going to happen—by gyrating his hips.

When we finally broke up in an embrace, I returned home to see my sister Sheila.

She appeared content when she descended the stairs after an additional hour. "Julian is here, and I have no doubt that you two will fall in love." I knew we were going to be in love the moment she threw open the door to greet this artist. I had sex with Julian, and because I was infatuated, I made a wild assumption that he would turn into a lion shifter like myself. It was beyond me how I was going to explain this to my sister, but perhaps I didn't have to.

We quickly came to the conclusion that we were meant to be together, and after noticing the expression in our eyes, my sister chose to disappear. I doubt we would communicate for a while, and when I told Julian that we were shifters, he was really surprised. At least we were together, even though I knew he wouldn't accept it until it actually happened. I didn't even know this person was going to enter my life, but we shared a unique link.

After a few minutes, Fred was able to reconnect with the CIA. With a sigh of relief, my heart was pounding as I clutched my chest. "What's happening then?" I stated.

Fred appeared wary of me, even in that dire hour. He looked down at my fingers, as though I was still holding a gun. Pointing to the screen of his monitor, he continued, "Things are happening." "However, I'm not sure if I should tell you the specifics."

"I admit that I didn't dream what you said earlier," I turned my chair over to face him. "What you mentioned to me in the living room. What you informed me back when we Prior to the commencement of the full undertaking...

With a smile, Fred said, "I know what I said." But even though it was only a few hours ago, the situation was drastically different from what it is now. I was experiencing a kind of cycle. You are aware of how it operates.

This was Fred's sweet side. When he was friendly with me.At least polite. Kind of like Rebecca, the way she spoke and carried herself.

He mumbled, almost in distaste, "I do want you." But at this moment, I can't have you. At this moment, I don't want you. I have priorities to attend to. Please be aware that I communicate with the CIA. Drop it and go on. Allow me to handle things. Here, I'm the alpha man. Not thee.

I wanted to fight against my body, but I nodded. How could he keep me unaware and blind? How was he able to prevent me from learning such vital information? It startled me and simultaneously irritated and infuriated me. Considering all the obstacles I had to overcome to get to where I was employed, I didn't want to be seen as maybe being a traitor.

Indeed, a government quota played a role in my employment. However, in order to be eligible for the quota in the first place, you must fulfil certain standards. I was in the top 5% of my class when I graduated and had been involved in various undergrad organisations that promoted human and werewolf peacekeeping.

How could I demonstrate that my interests aligned with his? Did I have to get down on my hands and knees? Offer myself as a subject and slave? Give up on my ability to think at all?

"All right," I murmured, giving up. I reclined in my chair, apprehensive and uneasy about what lay ahead. Thoughts of random possibilities about how things may go wrong for us started to proliferate, replicating like bacteria or viruses. For example, they could bomb the building, and I could collapse beneath a mound of rubble and stop breathing. suffocate in the flames and dust they would start.

It's not personal, according to Fred. "I don't want to take it personally, at least not right now. I just need to be really cautious and ready for anything, even if that's not my aim. You do realise this, don't you?

I answered, irritated, "I can." However, I would like to assist in any manner that I can. Can't you see that I desire to excel in my line of work?

Fred stated, "Trust is earned, not given." "I'm unable to make any more allowances. Just that one.

Giving in. As though my belief was all I needed or wanted.

"All right," I stated. "Do as you please. Be wary and suspicious of me despite the fact that I have only defended you. I turned my back on him just a little bit to express how uncomfortable I was. In a fleeting glimpse, he extended his hand to shake mine, but I declined.

"That's right," Fred replied, returning to his keyboard to continue typing. The angry, shouting part of him had settled and was no longer active. I detected a distinct type of animosity, one stemming from fatigue and incredulity. "You must allow me to go about things my way. Here, I'm in charge, not you. Didn't we just discuss this earlier?

"Comprehensive," I replied, unwilling to continue. "I fully comprehend,"

It felt like thirty minutes passed before there was any additional activity. I heard a lot of screaming and yelling coming from the lower levels below. There was an explosion that rocked the entire structure, followed by gunfire. My chair rolled across the room and slipped out from beneath me as I landed against the desk. I gripped the edge and stood back up, staring at Fred in disbelief.

Fred remarked, "It could be another round of attacks." "We ought to get ready. Take this from me.

He pulled out a revolver and gave it to me. Because it was semiautomatic, I felt a little more confident than I had previously.

Was he putting his life in my hands?

Or was there nothing else he could have done?

Was it the other way around?

He remarked, "Don't think too highly of yourself." "We must attend to our own mission. given that mine was cut short. Henley and Rebecca were supposed to rendezvous with us, or at least with me. They've been shortened, though. There is lockdown on the Angola. The ground floor is under CIA jurisdiction. However, we must eliminate the intermediate levels—from this point onward to them.

I raised an eyebrow. I had a small build and wasn't particularly built. I'm a twink, not a bear, not muscular, not anything else that most gay men would characterise me as. It was one thing to take out a few guys in the living room and hallway. But wiping out whole floors? That was a chore best left to a really strong person. not a person with my level of training.

Furthermore, I mean very, very little when I say some.

"Hold behind me," he commanded. "Aim not to stray too far."

"No problem," I replied. "You have my following."

Fred changed, a big blunderbuss between his jaws, one of those weapons werewolves used when they changed into wolves. I observed him rummaging through different paper sheets in an attempt to find something.

a box of ammunition. With me by his side, he slung it over his shoulders and under his stomach and made his way to the doorway.

"Okay, here we go," I murmured, not quite persuaded that I would be safe but confident that we would be saved in the end. I didn't think that humans could get away with being nasty all the time; I found it very hard to even imagine.

Fred padded out of the doorway and into the corridor, and I saw how much blood was on the floor as I followed. It seeped into the tiles and flowed inside from the outside like rivers. There had been arguing that had made me want to give up and cry all the way to my room.

even throw up.

I'd never seen so much before.

"I'm right behind you," I corrected myself. I had to remain present and committed to what we were doing at all times.

We entered the WIA head office through the front door and followed the stairway to the third floor. Even with our best efforts at squinting, we managed to make out what was on the other side, where a series of brilliant lights suspended on thick chains pelted us.

It would be an understatement to say that my parents and I have not always had an easy relationship. Their goals and ideals for me never quite matched my needs and desires. Their kid parading around a homosexual nightclub half-dressed to make a living is something they disapprove of, and they never understood the anguish I went through in college. exact words from my dad. Having children, taking care of the house, and supporting my dad in everything he does, even his opinions, my mom has always been my dad's ideal little omega.

Even though it's difficult for me to do, I pick up the phone and give my mum a call before starting dinner. Since she's the one person I know who is actually the greatest cook, I want everything to be flawless. I suppose I'm also experiencing some nostalgia, as I seem to recall the value of the clan and family.

It's been a while since I've phoned, so she probably thinks something is really wrong for me to actually pick up the phone and call her. She seems anxious and bewildered when I pick up the phone. I truly can't contain or stop myself when she asks me if something is wrong, even though it might be the wrong choice. I tell her the entire tale, apologising for my bad cooking and for not making the dinner I had promised Andrew. It's a lot to process, I know. Half of me wants her to hang up and act like I never phoned at all. I wait for nothing more than quiet to come from the other end of the queue.

"Honey, we'll start there. I remember Andrew always loved my meatloaf, so it will take more than one phone call to learn everything you need to know." She tells me to bring out a pencil and paper and write down the ingredients list and the directions for the meatloaf, corn and mashed potatoes, and I exhale with relief. My mom's cuisine makes my mouth swim, and I know Andrew will like it just as much. At my house, he always especially enjoyed mealtimes. His mother's meals frequently came from a box because she had a career to support.

I make a fast trip to the grocery, get everything I need, and go to work slicing the potatoes and assembling the meatloaf. By the time he gets here, I want the supper mostly done. As I labour, I consider how much has changed in a mere twenty-four hours. I never imagined that Andrew would return and that I would ever feel content or at ease in my life. I now understand the correlation between the two. I guess Andrew has always been my home, so I can finally relax now that he's back in my life and I know he feels the same way I do. Now that I have him in my life, I can finally breathe. Andrew isn't supposed to arrive for another ten minutes, so I have a steaming supper on the stove after two hours of intense focus. I yell,

"Shit," and Stonewall must have seen it as a challenge because he starts to bark and run in circles while I frantically attempt to figure out what to wear—anything not basketball shorts and a holey t-shirt, mind you—and my hair is a complete mess. I use my fingers to comb my hair before putting on a pair of slim trousers and a basic purple button-up shirt. I glance in the mirror at myself and meet its gaze. I deserve to be loved, truly and completely. I'm more than just a plaything or someone's punching bag.

I glance at myself in the mirror one more time before answering the doorbell when it rings. I tell Stonewall to be a good guy because he is pursuing me. When I open the door, I hope

Andrew is as excited as I am about what I have prepared for him.

Grant and Daniel climbed wearily up the porch's few steps. With a loud yawn, Daniel collapsed onto the couch and thumped his boots onto the coffee table.

"That was different," Grant sighed. "I didn't know you were capable of such violence. It appeared as though you were fully aware of his next move.

"To be honest, neither did I," Daniel said. However, considering what he did to Tabitha and you... I was angry, you know? Never before have I felt like that. It resembled... a mission.

"A goal," Grant mutely uttered.

"Just that!" Daniel concurred. To me, sparring has always seemed absurd. There was no reason to triumph.

"Well, you've never had anything to fight for really."

That's also what Tabitha mentioned. However, I do now.

With a content smile on his face, Grant fixed him with his gaze. Daniel felt the heat of his love radiating from his body.

However, he stole your ear!

Daniel attempted to chuckle. Gingerly, he touched the gauze bandage. "I know I look silly, don't I?"

"A few battle scars are appropriate for an Alpha."

He also has a good hold on you. "How's that rib doing?"

With hesitation, Grant lifted his arm and flinched. "I think I'm still pretty screwed up."

Feeling the skin beneath Grant's tight t-shirt, Daniel slid his palm over it.

Although there was still some healing in the area of the rib, he couldn't help but be amazed at how far Grant had gone in such a short amount of time. He could feel his manhood stirring, despite himself.

Grant took note of the bulge that was developing and smiled gratefully.

Daniel whispered, pulling in close to nuzzle Grant's strong jaw. "I can't help it."

Grant took a long breath, taking in the aroma of Daniel's blood as well as his musk. Lightning-fast impulses of yearning raced through his body in response. His passion surged as he felt Daniel's trailing fingers brush across his ribs.

He shoved Daniel down into the couch and put his own hand over his mouth, without caring about the pain. They made contact, and relief swept through him like a wave. It was at that very time that he realised how thirsty he had been for his lover's taste.

He was overcome with appreciation and affection as he recollected his desperate cry, his sense that it was useless, and his belief that he would perish in the cave. Though he was certain that the pack would continue without him, he was afraid for Daniel and was saddened by the thought of Daniel being by himself. Then, just when his hope was about to die, he miraculously heard Daniel's wolf in the soul-space. Somehow his mate had found him, something he would never have thought. Wonder and joy filled his heart.

He mumbled, "You saved me," into Daniel's hair, attempting to express his appreciation and amazement.

Daniel nodded and looked honestly in affection into his eyes. He murmured, feeling love rise up in his chest, "You saved me too."

Grant pressed hot, moist kisses all over Daniel's lips, each one more forceful than the last. With every second that went by, Daniel could feel Grant getting harder and harder. He took hold of his hips and forcefully pulled Grant onto his stomach, allowing him to feel the massive cock pulsating.

He heard himself groan, "I want you." It was amazing he could speak at all because he was so overcome with want.

Grant got up without thinking, unbuttoning his dark jeans and letting them drop on the ground. Daniel watched with hunger as his massive cock lunged forward, ready to get soaked.

Grant playfully swatted Daniel's hand away as he went down to touch his fly.

With a seductive half-smile, his lip curled as he growled, "Let me do that." Grant threw his jeans aside, pulling them over his slim hips as Daniel withdrew his hands.

Daniel pleaded, "Kiss me." Grant positioned his body over Daniel, sensing a searing electrical explosion connect to every millimetre of skin. He became lustfully hungry for Daniel's body at once, driven by the heat from their touch. Daniel moaned in want as he was kissed passionately, with him biting and sucking at his tongue. He leaned his weight on his forearms and delighted in the sensation of his thick chest hair gently brushing Daniel's massive abs and pecs as Daniel trembled with increasing excitement. He stroked his hips till Daniel started to moan, feeling Daniel's cock hardening desperately against his own.

Daniel felt that he could not become any more vicious, and his inner wolf was pleading for Grant to enter him. He enjoyed the sparks that shot out of his skull with every delightful instant of friction as he elevated his leg for leverage and drove his erection against Grant's rock-hard flesh.

Grant's climax flared in his balls, and he took a short breath. He made an effort to control it, but he knew it would only take a few seconds. He lowered himself to shove Daniel's leg against the couch and then straightened himself with a hand. Daniel raised his hips in an earnest nod, biting his lip.

Grant stroked Daniel's slick pre-cum all the way down to his ass, sliding the head of his cock along his taint. Daniel took a deep breath, longing to feel Grant complete him inside. He laced his fingers around Grant's neck and dragged him down in a long, deep kiss while Grant pushed hard on his ass. He aggressively inserted his tongue inside Grant's mouth.

Grant made an effort to be tactful and refrain, but his cock insisted on being in his partner. Daniel lost control as he was kissing him, thrusting deeper and quicker at first.

With each long, deep push, Daniel felt Grant's buttocks clench as he hooked his leg behind them. He pressed his erection against Grant's muscular, hairy tummy as Grant plunged his cock in him.

Grant opened his eyes, his heart pounding more and more, and looked directly at Daniel.

He yelled, "Look at me!" with urgency. An strong avalanche of passion threatened to drown Daniel, but he forced himself to open his eyes. He pulled Grant hard into him as he gazed into his eyes and felt the orgasmic spiral slow down to a blinding pace.

As Grant reached his peak, he gasped and buried his cock in a deep, demanding push, staying there the entire time as his balls discharged sperm wave after cum wave into Daniel. Daniel felt his release, pouring hot, pearly come between their stomachs and looking deeply into Grant's eyes as his orgasm peaked and climaxed.

Grant landed hard on his face and buried it in Daniel's neck. He kissed his lover's sweaty jaw with gratitude as a wellspring of joy that nearly brought him to tears.

Awestruck, he mumbled into Daniel's hair, "You are my Alpha."

Daniel gave Grant a deep hug and showered him with praise while their wolves danced happily in the soul-space.

Overcome with love, he muttered back, "And you are my Alpha."

"Eternally."

Caster felt Simon's silky lips wrap over his rock-hard cock, and he fought, but failed, to contain his groan of delight. He was astounded to find that he could actually feel Simon's mouth around him as he watched as inch after inch of him vanished down into his throat.

"Simon, fuck off. He moaned, wrapping his hand around Simon's head to pull him in closer. "That feels so good," he said. Caster had felt, up until now, that he had failed to impress him.

Warm and velvety around his cock, Simon's mouth took him down voraciously, every inch vanishing into his throat. Caster moaned, "God, I've wanted this so bad." "Simon, I also need to taste you." He forced Simon to turn over on his back on the table after removing himself from his mouth. Simon's robe had already become too big around his belt, and the front sprang out to show off his firm manhood. Caster pulled the robe completely open and drew his face closer to Simon's silky, pink dick, saying, 'You look fucking delicious, Simon'. With a satisfied flick of his tongue across his skull, he caused Simon's body to tremble.

Then, in an attempt to enjoy Simon and himself simultaneously, Caster leaped onto the table and threw himself over him. Caster tucked Simon's penis deep down his mouth, tasting his omega flavour as he ravenously ate it. Though he didn't need to, he was unable to see what Simon was doing. He experienced Simon's tongue trailing down the length of his cock, first from tip to base, then rising up around his balls. He felt him softly suck on his balls, taking them into his mouth one at a time.

With his nose inches from his opening, Caster could smell Simon's fertility as he swallowed his cock. He questioned whether Simon was still aware of what would happen to an omega if an alpha's seed were to fill him up. How was he able to know? When he found out, how would he respond?

He needed to tell him, but not at this moment.

He pulled away from Simon and, using a powerful hand, threw him onto his stomach, bending him over the table with his ass open and willing. Caster could sense Simon's intense need. He took out a condom from the nearby dresser and unfolded it onto his torso. Simon turned to face him again.

"That's not necessary to use," he stated. "I don't care if you give it to me raw."

Caster took a little break. He thought better of it than to rip the condom off his cock, pour his semen into him, and then deal with the fallout. He gave a headshake. "You'll have to work for that," he grinned.

I must inform him.

Squeezing one of Simon's silky ass cheeks with his palm, he felt its shapeliness and warmth in his hand before opening him up. He held his sheathed cock right in front of Simon's opening, feeling the heat of need radiating onto his dick as he did so. His cock throbbed. Caster grunted as his cock slowly sank into Simon as Simon slid backwards in his body.